THE IMPORTANCE OF MEDITATION

A Christian Guide To Transform Your Thought Life

Isaac Samuel II

Copyright © 2020 by Isaac Samuel Ministries Intl.

All rights reserved. No part of this publication may be reproduced, distributed or transmitted in any form or by any means, without prior written permission.

Isaac Samuel Ministries Intl.
711 Flatbush Ave
Brooklyn, NY 11225
www.pastorsamuel.org

Scripture quotes taken from the Holy Bible, New Living Translation (NLT) – Copyright © 1996, 2004, 2007, 2015 by Tyndale House Foundation. Used by permission of Tyndale House Publishers, Inc.

Unless otherwise noted, all Scripture quotations are from the King James Version Bible (KJV) -Public Domain

ISBN 978-1-7345653-5-5

ACKNOWLEDGMENTS

First, I must thank My Heavenly Father, who is the real author of this book, the One I serve, and the Source of my life. He's my Helper, Inspiration, and my All in All. I give Him all the glory for this project.

I thank my beloved wife, Pastor Christabel, and our beautiful children, Rex, Divine, and Ivana, for the tremendous sacrifices they have made while I was busy about My Father's business.

Special thanks to my parents, Dr. and Mrs. I. I. Samuel, and grandparents — notably my grandfathers, Bishop A.N.C. Iyalla and Reverend Isaac Obu Samuel, who prayed and gave me their blessings for ministry.

I also want to appreciate the members of Check It Church International, especially my loyal assistant, Kebrina Robinson, who has been of immense help and support.

Thank you all for your kind words, thoughts, and prayers. God bless you.

Contents

Acknowledgments iii

Introduction v

1. We Are in Perilous Times 1
2. Is Good Cheer Even Possible? 4
3. Times of Persecution and Tribulations 10
4. Understanding and Receiving Through Meditation 14
5. There Are Rules 17
6. There's Preparation in Meditation 19
7. Changes Are Coming 25
8. You Have a Role to Play 28
9. Meditate with a Shout 36
10. Seeing is Achieving 39
11. Meditation Shows You the Depth of God's Love 45
12. Stand Firm 50

INTRODUCTION

This book was written with clarity and simplicity to teach you about the importance of meditation in your Christian walk.

The Bible states in Joshua 1:8, "This book of the law shall not depart out of thy mouth; but thou shalt meditate therein day and night, that thou mayest observe to do according to all that is written therein: for then thou shalt make thy way prosperous, and then thou shalt have good success."

This scripture, along with several others in the Bible, shows that God expects us not only to read and hear His words but to meditate on them as well. Unfortunately, many Christians do not know that they ought to meditate, and, as a result, they fail to benefit from the deeper things of the Spirit.

The Hebrew word for meditation originated from two separate root words. The first is hagah, which means "to utter in a low sound," and the second is siach, which implies "to be occupied with" or "concerned about." In simpler terms, meditation means repetitious pondering of God's Word and speaking to yourself about it.

An excellent example of mediation is The Battle of Jericho in Joshua 6. In the quest to win Canaan, God instructed Joshua to have his army march silently around Jericho once a day for six straight days and, after seven rounds on the seventh day, to shout. The Israelites did as instructed, and after the final circuit, the men produced a mighty roar, and Jericho's walls miraculously fell.

How did this happen?
Meditation!
The quiet march before this scream was a form of meditation. Hallelujah!

The constant recollection of God's Word and repetition of thought guarantee success. In this book, you will receive a clear understanding of meditation and how you can apply it to produce good results.

• CHAPTER 1 •

We Are in Perilous Times

"These things I have spoken unto you, that in me ye might have peace. In the world ye shall have tribulation: but be of good cheer; I have overcome the world." John 16:33

We are living in perilous times, and we need the Word of God now, more than ever. All over the media and even in private conversations, there are discussions about growing terrorist threats, failing economies, and the possibility of a third world war.

Adding insult to injury, the increased competition among cable news outlets has driven us into a permanent state of panic and pandemonium. Their misguided efforts to continuously inform the public about disastrous world affairs have only heightened fear and mistrust.

As Christians, none of these recent calamities should surprise us. In John 16:33, Jesus told us that we would face tribulations in this world. What we are witnessing are signs of the times. We are in the very last days, and in all honesty, it is not going to get any better. If anyone tells you that things will improve, they are lying to you. There will be more dire news stories, more economic problems, and more senseless killings.

The great news is that the verse did not end with tribulations. Jesus went on to say, "Be of good cheer, I have overcome the world."
Hallelujah!

This verse implies that just as He overcame the world, so can we.

Rejoice, there is hope!

• CHAPTER 2 •

Is Good Cheer Even Possible?

Some of you are probably asking yourself if it is possible to be of good cheer under these circumstances. The answer is: absolutely and undoubtedly, yes! We can be of good cheer, and I will tell you how.

Do you remember the Parable of the Sower?

Matthew 13:1–23

"The same day went Jesus out of the house, and sat by the sea side. 2 And great multitudes were gathered together

unto him, so that he went into a ship, and sat; and the whole multitude stood on the shore. 3 And he spake many things unto them in parables, saying, Behold, a sower went forth to sow; 4 And when he sowed, some seeds fell by the way side, and the fowls came and devoured them up: 5 Some fell upon stony places, where they had not much earth: and forthwith they sprung up, because they had no deepness of earth: 6 And when the sun was up, they were scorched; and because they had no root, they withered away. 7 And some fell among thorns; and the thorns sprung up, and choked them: 8 But other fell into good ground, and brought forth fruit, some an hundredfold, some sixtyfold, some thirtyfold. 9 Who hath ears to hear, let him hear."

In verse 18, Jesus began to explain the meaning of the parable:

"18 Hear ye therefore the parable of the sower. 19 When any one heareth the Word of the kingdom, and understandeth it not, then cometh the wicked one, and catcheth away that which was sown in his heart. This is he which received seed by the way side. 20 But he that received the seed into stony places, the same is he that heareth the Word, and anon with joy receiveth it; 21 Yet hath he not root in himself, but dureth for a while: for when tribulation or persecution ariseth because of

the Word, by and by he is offended. 22 He also that received seed among the thorns is he that heareth the Word; and the care of this world, and the deceitfulness of riches, choke the Word, and he becometh unfruitful. 23 But he that received seed into the good ground is he that heareth the Word, and understandeth it; which also beareth fruit, and bringeth forth, some an hundredfold, some sixty, some thirty."

Now, although I'm speaking to all Christians, I believe the largest beneficiary of this message will be those who fall into 'the seed on rocky soil' category. Here, the Word is immediately received with great joy. They are often the ones who continually shout in church, *"Preach, Pastor, preach!"* But when pressured, they quickly succumb because the Word does not have roots in them.

It's not enough for us to shout and dance in church. We must personalize the Word so that it registers in our thoughts and behaviors.

One sure way of personalizing the Word is through meditation.

You must ask yourself,

"Do I believe that God can do all things? Do I have faith that there is nothing too hard for Him? Do I truly believe that He is who He said He is?"

If you answer with a definite "yes," then you should brace yourself. Let me be as straightforward as possible; when the Word comes to you, it also attracts tribulation and persecution. Jesus says persecution arises because of the Word, and that's why we must get to that position where we hold on to God's Word against all the odds.

It doesn't matter what you hear or how you feel; you must stand in faith. The definition of faith in Hebrews 11:1 is, *"Now faith is the substance of things hoped for, the evidence of things not seen."*

My simplified definition of faith is, *"God said it. I believe it, and that settles it."*

It is essential to have a clear understanding of your level of faith because in the scriptures, the enemy always tries to dispute the Word of God.

When God told Adam and Eve not to eat from the Tree of the Knowledge of Good and Evil or they would die that day, Satan showed up and issued a challenge: "Has God Said?" – Satan disputes the Word.

John the Baptist baptized Jesus at the Jordan. The Bible says the Spirit of God came down upon him as a dove and said, *"This is My beloved Son, in whom I am well pleased."* Matthew 3:17

God spoke audibly. Jesus heard it, John heard it, but guess what the next chapter of the Bible says? Jesus was driven into the wilderness to be tempted by the devil.

What was the first thing the devil said to him? *"If thou be the Son of God, command that these stones be made bread."* Matthew 4:3 – The devil disputes and contends with the Word of God.

Whenever God speaks, it attracts tribulation and persecution. Whenever God speaks, the devil is attracted. He aims to dispute the Word of God and to fight against what God has told you.

That's why no matter what you see or feel, you have to stand on God's Word.

God said, "You're healed," but you still feel some pain. Remain firm and declare, "God said it. I believe it, and that settles it!"

God said, "I have set before you an open door, and no man can shut it," but it looks like you're blocked at every turn. Hold on and affirm, "God said it. I believe it, and that settles it!"

You received a prophecy that you will have your baby, but two years have passed and there is still no sign of conception. Don't give up. Stand strong and shout, "God said it. I believe it, and that settles it!"

• CHAPTER 3 •

Times of Persecution and Tribulations

Amidst persecutions and tribulations, the cowardly enemy will show up with his bag of deceptions. He will try to convince you that God lied to give you false hope. However, as with seeds that are planted in good soil, we know there's no such thing as false hope in Christ. The Bible says in Colossians 1:27, *"Christ in you, the hope of glory."* So, rest assured. As long as Christ is in you, His promises will come to pass.

For those who are not rooted, He says, *"when affliction or persecution ariseth for the word's sake, immediately they are offended."*

What does it mean when Jesus says he's offended? Is he offended because he's angry? No! It means he begins to deviate from the way and change his confession. He loses the ground of God's will and the Word that was planted into him. And so, the seed is choked and dies.

For those that received seed among the thorns, He says *"is he that heareth the word; and the care of this world, and the deceitfulness of riches, choke the word, and he becometh unfruitful."*

Did you see that?

He said He received the Word, but the cares of this world and the deceitfulness of riches smothered it. Many people have the opinion that having a particular item or person in their lives would make life worth living. That is the deceitfulness of riches!

The Bible says in 1 Timothy 6:6–7, *"Godliness with contentment is great gain. For we brought nothing into this world, and it is certain we can carry nothing out."* God expects you to be content with the level you're on.

Be happy. Be satisfied. If what you have now is all that God has blessed you with, be grateful to Him.

Be thankful!

When you're not grateful, the cares of this life will consume you, and that usually comes with temptations.

The devil knows that the Word will grow undisturbed if it is sown into your heart, and your heart is a fertile ground. He knows that if you can only believe the Word and keep saying the Word to yourself against all odds, eventually, the Word of God will come to pass in your life.

And so he does everything to fight the Word. His fight is not with you; it's with the Word because he knows if it is inside of you, it will produce results.

Matthew 13:23 reads, *"But he that received seed into the good ground is he that heareth the Word, and understandeth it; which also beareth fruit, and bringeth forth, some an hundredfold, some sixty, some thirty."* Here it is in plain view; the devil knows that if the Word of God gains ground in your heart and you understand the Word, he can't stop you!

So, here we have the seed which fell by the wayside, and the devil was able to steal the Word. The one that fell among the stony ground, which eventually died. The one that fell among thorns which choked and the one that fell on good soil.

What's the difference? The difference is simply receiving the Word and understanding the Word through meditation.

• CHAPTER 4 •

Understanding and Receiving Through Meditation

It's not enough for you to go to church and hear a sermon. There are different levels of meditation, and that why Jesus said, *"... some an hundredfold, some sixty, some thirty."* The more you meditate on the Word, the more fruitful you become.

Studies show people only remember about 10 percent of what they hear. I have personally tested this theory and found after speaking for one hour, audience members were only able to articulate a sliver of what was said. Their receptivity had very little to do with the subject matter or the environment but the human brain's ability to retain enormous amounts of information.

As I enter my twelfth year as a pastor, I must say I'm thankful for the advancement in technology. With YouTube, Facebook Live, and a wide variety of phone recording apps, you now have the opportunity to replay messages when convenient. With these devices, every time you repeat a message, you hear something new, and your brain is more receptive. More importantly, your heart also hears the Word, and it eventually gets into your Spirit. Then the Word becomes a revelation; it becomes part of your thoughts and your life.

According to The American Journal of Clinical Nutrition, a child's physical growth and health are directly related to their food intake.

For example, if someone's parents are tall, naturally, they would also be above-average height.

However, if the person continually eats the wrong foods, their poor diet will stunt their growth.

In other words, people are the way they are because of the food that they digest.

This analogy is the same for spiritual food. When you go to church and you hear the sermon, it's like eating. The more you ingest, the more of God's Word you digest. Just keep in mind, the level of digestion is parallel to your level of meditation. The higher the meditation, the greater the result in your life.

• CHAPTER 5 •

There Are Rules

We have a lot of people claiming to be God's generals, but that does not mean it's true. After all, anyone can give themselves a title. In countries where rebel groups fight against the government, the rebel leader calls himself a general, but that doesn't make him one.
A title must and should be accompanied by a mantle for you to be effective at anything. You have a responsibility, and there are certain things that you have to do.

The Word has to abide in you if you want to be called a child of God. Jesus said in John 15:4, "Abide in me, and I in you. As the branch cannot bear fruit of itself, except it abide in the vine; no more can ye, except ye abide in me."

I started our conversation by saying we are living in perilous times, and here Jesus is telling us that only those that abide in the Word will be able to stand in these times.

Webster's dictionary defines the word 'abide' as an act in accordance with a rule. It is synonymous with the terms obey, observe, follow, uphold, heed, and accept. In John 15:4, Jesus is clearly explaining the importance of connecting to Him – our vine.

The fruit that Jesus speaks of is simply evidence of a relationship with Him. It is a relationship that He initiates through and by His love for us and one that we maintain through meditation.

• CHAPTER 6 •

There's Preparation in Meditation

The Word of God is the manual of our lives, and His intentions are evident in how He prepares us.

In Isaiah 60:1, God says, *"Arise, shine; for thy light is come, and the glory of the LORD is risen upon thee."*

What is light?

God's Word is light!

The Bible states, *"Thy word is a lamp unto my feet, and a light unto my path."* Psalm 119:105.

Psalm 119:130 says, *"The entrance of thy words giveth light; it giveth understanding unto the simple."*

So why is God urging us to arise and shine?

The urgency has everything to do with preparation. In the next verse, He says, *"For, behold, the darkness shall cover the earth, and gross darkness the people: but the Lord shall arise upon thee, and his glory shall be seen upon thee."*

Immediately after, God talks about the light coming and the glory rising; He mentions the Darkness. He doesn't just say "darkness," He says "the Darkness."

He's talking about a personality.

He's talking about a person: the devil.

In the previous chapters, I warned you that the devil likes to contend with God's Word.

His modus operandi is the same; the devil always shows up after the Word of God is released.

A perfect example was Adam and Eve in the Book of Genesis. God warned them not to eat from the Tree of the Knowledge of Good and Evil for they would surely die.

The devil immediately came and whispered to Eve, *"God deceived you."*

Imagine the liar himself and the father of lies calling God a deceiver—and Eve fell for it!

Why? Because the Word was not rooted.

The moment you take your eyes, ears, or mind off God and start listening to that other voice, trouble will come.

In the end, the only people who will stand are those who allow God's Word to gain ground in their hearts. Isaiah 60:2 says, *"But the Lord shall arise upon thee, and his glory shall be seen upon thee."*

When you meditate on the Word, people will begin to ask you, "How are you still cool, calm, and collected when all these things are happening around the world?"

The secret is meditation!

I want to show you something interesting in Acts 27. This chapter depicts the time when Apostle Paul was imprisoned for breaking Jewish laws. The people called for his death as punishment, but as a Roman citizen, he appealed to Caesar, and the soldiers were tasked to take him to Rome.

On their journey to Rome, they encountered extreme winds, which made sailing difficult. While seeking shelter in a place called Safe Harbors, near the city of Lasea, Paul warned them, *"Men, I can see that there will be a lot of trouble on this trip. The ship, everything in it, and even our lives may be lost!"* But the captain and the owner of the ship did not agree with Paul.

A few hours after resuming their journey, a terrible storm arose and began to toss the ship violently. For many days, they were unable to see the sun or the moon. The men started losing hope of staying alive, and many lost their appetite.

Then one day, Paul stood up before them and said, *"Men, I told you not to leave Crete. You should have listened to me. Then you would not have all this trouble and loss. But now I tell you to be of good cheer. None of you will die, but the ship will be lost. Last night an angel came to me from God—the God I worship and belong to. The angel said, 'Paul, don't be afraid! You must stand before Caesar. And God has given you this promise: He will save the lives of all those sailing with you.' So men, there is nothing to worry about. I trust God, and I am sure everything will happen just as his angel told me. But we will crash on an island."* Acts 27: 21–26

Can you imagine how the soldiers and sailors on the ship felt? They checked their weather forecast, and everything looked good, but then this storm blindsided them. But Paul was not caught unawares because he had information from the Holy Spirit, and he was confident that no one was going to die.

Why was Paul so confident?

Verse 23 stated that an angel came to him from God and said, *"Paul, don't be afraid! You must stand before Caesar. And God has given you this promise: He will save the lives of all those sailing with you."*

Hallelujah! Glory to God!

The Word of the Lord came to him, giving him confidence even though everybody was worried. The men on the ship were anxious about the situation, but Paul remained calm because he had received information from God. He was confident! Paul knew it was not his time to die because the Word had come to him.

Remember, I said that in the end, the only people who will stand are those who allow the Word of God to gain ground in their hearts – and that is why you must take the Word of God more seriously if you want to make it in these last days.

• CHAPTER 7 •

Changes Are Coming

It's no secret that there are plans for a new world order – a One-World Government. The time is quickly approaching when the economy and everything around us is going to change.

When we were kids, we heard about a cashless society. We thought it was a joke, but it's happening right before our eyes.

Now, even in third-world countries, there are ATMs everywhere. When I was growing up in Nigeria, I heard travelers talk about ATMs in America and Europe. A machine where you could go any time of the day and take money out – I thought that was a joke.

I thought, well, that could only happen in that part of the world. It can never happen in Africa. Now there are ATMs across the continent.

We have become a digital world. To book a stay in a hotel, you must use a credit card. Even job and college applications are now completed online. We are fast entering a cashless society, and all the things that the Word of God said would happen are coming to pass.

We're in the last days!

I know you've heard this since you were a child, and now you're an adult, and the world keeps going.

Let me remind you that the Bible says a thousand days before God is like an evening. That's not because God is slow concerning what he said; He's trying to allow more people to come in.

That's why he's doing it, but that doesn't mean we are not in the last days.

It's interesting to see how some people have received end times messages. Some try to estimate the time—*maybe it's going to be 30 years from now, so I will enjoy my life for 25 or 28 years and then give my life to Christ.*

The question is, who promised you tomorrow? The day you die, the world has ended for you, and you are going to meet your maker and face eternity.

Whether the world comes to an end or you come to an end, something is coming to an end.

And that's why we have to be prepared because only those rooted and grounded in the Word would stay.

There will be a great shaking in the last days, and everything that you believe will be questioned, but the key to surviving is meditating on the Word of God.

CHAPTER 8

You Have a Role to Play

I often say God is a businessman and rightfully so. All promises of God come with conditions, and there are things we must do if we want to see their manifestation. In other words, for the promises of God to be visible in your life, you have to play a role.

Let us take a look at the book of Joshua. There's something very interesting in the first chapter. The story begins after Moses has died and Joshua has become the leader of the Israelites.

Joshua 1:1–9

"1 Now after the death of Moses the servant of the Lord it came to pass, that the Lord spake unto Joshua the son of Nun, Moses' minister, saying, 2 Moses my servant is dead; now therefore arise, go over this Jordan, thou, and all this people, unto the land which I do give to them, even to the children of Israel. 3 Every place that the sole of your foot shall tread upon, that have I given unto you, as I said unto Moses. 4 From the wilderness and this Lebanon even unto the great river, the river Euphrates, all the land of the Hittites, and unto the great sea toward the going down of the sun, shall be your coast. 5 There shall not any man be able to stand before thee all the days of thy life: as I was with Moses, so I will be with thee: I will not fail thee, nor forsake thee. 6 Be strong and of a good courage: for unto this people shalt thou divide for an inheritance the land, which I sware unto their fathers to give them. 7 Only be thou strong and very courageous, that thou mayest observe to do according to all the law, which Moses my servant commanded thee: turn not from it to the right hand or to the left, that thou mayest prosper whithersoever thou goest. 8 This book of the law shall not

depart out of thy mouth; but thou shalt meditate therein day and night, that thou mayest observe to do according to all that is written therein: for then thou shalt make thy way prosperous, and then thou shalt have good success. 9 Have not I commanded thee? Be strong and of good courage; be not afraid, neither be thou dismayed: for the Lord thy God is with thee whithersoever thou goest."

At the beginning of the chapter, we saw God reiterating to Joshua the promise He made to Moses; however, He required that the people be strong and courageous.

Why was this requirement so important?

You see, sometimes we overlook some critical instructions because they seem frivolous, but to God, they are huge things.

For example, I always feel a certain way when I hear Christians making statements like *"I'm discouraged."* Some think they are genuinely expressing themselves, but God said to be strong and courageous. So they are actually showing disobedience by making statements like *"I'm discouraged."*

One fundamental way to avoid making erroneous statements and actions is meditation. Many people hear the Word, but their reception of what they hear is the key.

God said to Joshua, *"The only thing I want you to do is to be strong and courageous."* So from today, do not use words like *"I'm weak."* God said to be strong!

When He talks about strength, He's not talking about your physical strength. You could be weak in the flesh, but never be weak in the Spirit.

Do you remember what Jesus told his disciples in Gethsemane?

He said, *"The spirit is willing, but the flesh is weak."*

God understands that we're humans and that there will be a weakness of the flesh, but if we think the Spirit is weak, we admit weakness. Never admit weakness.

The truth is that anything paramount in your heart will sooner or later come out of your mouth. If all you read about is physics, and you are called upon to speak, you'll be discussing physics before you know it. This is the same for anything you dwell upon in your mind, including the Word of God.

THE IMPORTANCE OF MEDITATION

Joshua 1:8 reads, *"This book of the law shall not depart out of thy mouth; but thou shalt meditate therein day and night, that thou mayest observe to do according to all that is written therein: For then thou shalt make thy way prosperous, and then thou shalt have good success."*

What does it mean when He said we should meditate on it day and night?

It means to saturate yourself with the Word. Let the Word of God always be in what you listen to and read and in your conversations.

I mentioned in an earlier chapter that the devil always tries to contend with God's Word, and this is one of the main reasons why we must meditate. If you choose not to follow God's instructions and meditate on the Word day and night, that "other" voice will come!

The people of the world will suggest alternative meditation methods like yoga and chakra, but can darkness fight the darkness?

The answer is NO!

We live in a spiritual world, and we cannot prevent that "other" voice from coming, but we can stop the voice from staying.

For example, you can't stop a bird from flying over your head, no matter how hard you try, but you can certainly stop the bird from laying an egg on your head.

So when that "other" voice comes, you should be bold enough to rebuke it. Just like the master, Jesus, said, *"Get thee behind me, Satan, thou art an offense unto me."* Jesus knew how to put the devil in his place. He wasn't going to listen to that "other" voice. He was focused on the voice of God, and that should be our focus as well.

The second part of Joshua 1:8 says, *"that thou mayest observe to do according to all that is written therein: for then thou shalt make thy way prosperous, and then thou shalt have good success."*

If the Word of God is your meditation, it will also become your action. For instance, the Bible says, *"Seest thou a man diligent in his business? He shall stand before kings; he shall not stand before mean men."* Proverbs 22:29. If you meditate on that verse long enough, you will find yourself being diligent. There will be a supernatural urge to be attentive and persistent in all that you do.

The key is meditation.

You say it in your heart, sometimes you speak it out loud, and other times you shout the Word, but always say it.

One thing I've discovered over the years is that the devil never gives up. I've been born again for over two decades, filled with the Holy Spirit, and the devil still tries to fight my salvation. Ever so often, I would hear his sleazy voice accusing me, "are you sure you are born again?" You think he gets tired? No!

That's why you must remind yourself daily that you're a child of God, a chosen generation, a Royal Priesthood, a Holy Nation, and a peculiar people. 1 Peter 1:23 says, *"Being born again, not of corruptible seed, but of incorruptible, by the word of God, which liveth and abideth for ever."*

And this is what meditation is all about.

The Word states, *"This book of the law shall not depart out of thy mouth; but thou shalt meditate therein day and night, that thou mayest observe to do according to all that is written therein: for then thou shalt make thy way prosperous, and then thou shalt have good success."*

It did not say God will do it all by Himself. The scripture states, if you meditate on the Word, then thou shalt make thy way prosperous.

You have a role to play!

• CHAPTER 9 •

Meditate with a Shout

Three stages of meditation exist. The first stage is when you talk to yourself in your heart. In these times you're ruminating on the Word. The second stage is when you begin to verbalize it. And the third stage is when you start to shout the Word of God.

Some may ask, "What does shouting have to do with meditation?"

Let me tell you something; at some point during your life, you will need to shout. Learn to shout in your room; lock the door and scream. God gave us the ability to scream for a reason, so let the Word permeate the atmosphere.

Everyone knows that person who shouts in church—you know, the one everybody thinks is a fanatic or maybe overdoing it. Now, look at the ones who sit quietly and maintain their level. How is their life?

I'm speaking from experience. There is a time to think the Word, to speak the Word, and to shout the Word.

The Bible reads, *"The lion has roared—who will not fear?"* Amos 3:8

When you shout the Word, you truly begin to roar.

Start by shouting, "I've got victory!"

By the third shout, your victory will dawn on you.

Once the devil hears you shout, that coward will flee.

Joshua used meditation to bring down the walls of Jericho. In the quest to win Canaan, God instructed Joshua to have his army march silently around Jericho once a day for six straight days and, after seven rounds on the seventh day, to shout. The Israelites did as directed, and, after the final circuit, the men produced a mighty roar, and Jericho's walls miraculously fell.

How did this happen?

Meditation!

The march before the mighty roar was a form of meditation. The Israelites were quiet at first, but, in their hearts, they were saying, *"Jericho wall, I see you coming down. You're coming down."* And, when the time came for them to shout, they did, and the giant wall fell.

What's that Jericho wall in your life?

What's that thing standing in your way?

This is not the time to maintain your level; IT'S TIME TO SHOUT!

• CHAPTER 10 •

Seeing is Achieving

After Lot had gone, the Lord said to Abram, "Look as far as you can see in every direction—north and south, east and west. I am giving all this land, as far as you can see, to you and your descendants as a permanent possession."
Genesis 13:14–15 (NLT)

Sight is an integral part of meditation. I'm not referring to your optical eyes, but rather the eyes of your mind—your imagination.

Recently, I saw a man of God ministering to a demon-possessed man. The guy was manifesting, and the minster gave him a command to kneel, but the demon refused. In response to its defiance, the minister said, "*I see you kneeling now,*" and, before his sentence was complete, the man dropped to his knees.

How did the man of God achieve this result? Meditation!

By using his imagination, he went into the realm of the Spirit and got the man's knees to the ground.

Hallelujah!

Throughout the Bible, there were various instances where the power of meditation through sight and imagination was applied. Do you remember the story of the Tower of Babel?

Genesis 11:1–9

1 And the whole earth was of one language, and of one speech. 2 And it came to pass, as they journeyed from the east, that they found a plain in the land of Shinar; and they dwelt there. 3 And they said one to another, Go to, let us make brick, and burn them thoroughly. And they had brick for stone, and slime had they for morter. 4 And they said, Go to, let us build us a city and a tower, whose top may reach unto heaven; and let us make us a name, lest we be scattered abroad upon the face of the whole earth. 5 And the Lord came down to see the city and the tower, which the children of men builded. 6 And the Lord said, Behold, the people is one, and they have all one language; and this they begin to do: and now nothing will be restrained from them, which they have imagined to do. 7 Go to, let us go down, and there confound their language, that they may not understand one another's speech. 8 So the Lord scattered them abroad from thence upon the face of all the earth: and they left off to build the city. 9 Therefore is the name of it called Babel; because the Lord did there confound the language of all the earth: and from thence did the Lord scatter them abroad upon the face of all the earth.

Did you see that?

Verse six says, *"and now nothing will be restrained from them, which they have imagined to do."*

From the very beginning, it was God's intention for humankind to reproduce and multiply across the earth, but the people decided to stay together. Using their imaginative ability, they forged ahead to build the tower, and the only way for God to stop them was to confuse their language.

It's important to point out that these people were against the will of God. It was not God's plan for them to build the tower, but because their power of imagination was so strong, God said, *"nothing they set out to do will be impossible for them."* Genesis 11:6 (NLT)

Do you see the power of imagination?

Imagine how much more powerful it would be when you use your imagination in the will of God.

God will not stop you!

The devil certainly will not be able to stop you!

Nobody will be able to stop you!

The people of the world have been using meditation for a long time, and some are using it to do terrible things. When a person takes someone's picture or personal item to a voodoo priest or priestess, the witchcraft worker closes their eyes and makes incantations. That is a form of meditation—evil meditation—but meditation, nonetheless.

As a child of God, you also have that ability; the only difference is you will use it for good.

Begin to practice it. Let's say you've been feeling pain in your body. Close your physical eyes, and open the eyes of your mind. See yourself pain-free and speak God's promises of healing, *"Jehovah Rapha, you're the Lord that healeth. Lord, by Your stripes I'm healed. I receive strength in the name of Jesus...."*

If you can see with the eyes of your mind, it's only a matter of time until you begin to feel better. Hallelujah!

I want to draw your attention to 2 Corinthians 5:17. I'm sure you have read this scripture a hundred times before, but there's something significant that most people miss. The scripture says, *"Therefore, if any man be in Christ, he is a new creature: Old things are passed away; behold, all things are become new."*

Apostle Paul said, "BEHOLD, *all things are become new."* The Greek word for behold is *eídō*, which means to see, be aware, or perceive.

Do you see how important it is to see with the eyes of your mind?

Some Christians struggle with their past sins, but the Bible says, *"Behold, all things are become new."* If only they could grasp what this verse is saying, they would be free indeed.

Meditation is the key to seeing the achievable.
Revelation 3:8 reads, *"I know thy works: Behold, I have set before thee an open door, and no man can shut it."*

Can you see the open door before you? Every day, declare, *"I see the doors are opening. No barriers can stop me in the name of Jesus. Behold, I'm getting there. I now possess my possessions. I can see in the Spirit's realm, and it's mine in the name of Jesus. I see myself going through the open door!*

Oh, glory to God. I see it!"

• CHAPTER 11 •

Meditation Shows You the Depth of God's Love

If someone were to ask you to describe how much God loves you, would you be able to? Even if you spend the rest of your life describing His love for you, it will not be enough.

The love of God is pure; it's perfect and infinite in all its capacities. Sadly, many people take God's love for granted, and it's often over-simplified, trivialized, misunderstood, and misused. The secret to understanding the depth of God's love is to be rooted and grounded in the Word.

Apostle Paul, in a prayer written for the Ephesians, states, "*14 When I think of all this, I fall to my knees and pray to the Father, 15 the Creator of everything in heaven and on earth. 16 I pray that from his glorious, unlimited resources he will empower you with inner strength through his Spirit. 17 Then Christ will make his home in your hearts as you trust in him. Your roots will grow down into God's love and keep you strong. 18 And may you have the power to understand, as all God's people should, how wide, how long, how high, and how deep his love is. 19 May you experience the love of Christ, though it is too great to understand fully. Then you will be made complete with all the fullness of life and power that comes from God. 20 Now all glory to God, who is able, through his mighty power at work within us, to accomplish infinitely more than we might ask or think. 21 Glory to Him in the church and in Christ Jesus through all generations forever and ever! Amen"* Ephesians 3:14–21 (NLT)

To be rooted and grounded in God's love is to be rooted in the Word of God. As you meditate on God's Word, the love of God will be driven deeper into your heart, and you will get a clearer understanding of His love.

Verse 20 says, *"Now all glory to God, who is able, through his mighty power at work within us, to accomplish infinitely more than we might ask or think."*

What makes the power work in us?

Meditation!

You see, many Christians don't know that they have power because it's dormant. However, if you keep reminding yourself of who you are in Christ, that power will move from being dormant to being dominant. For instance, if you tell yourself, *"I can do all things through Christ, who strengthens me,"* you will be empowered from the inside, and ultimately, it will manifest on the outside.

Some years ago, I knew a guy who was on fire for God. At one point, he became a pastor and seemed to be deep in things of the Spirit. Recently, I heard that he's no longer a Christian and doesn't believe in God anymore.

How could something like that happen to somebody who was professing Christ?

The obvious answer is that he was not rooted and grounded in the Word. Somewhere along the way, challenges came and quenched his fire.

There are certain things that your pastor can do for you, and there are some things that only you can do for yourself.

How much of God's Word do you intake daily? How much of God do you consume? If you are ruminating on the Word, you will not be among those that fall away from the faith. Instead, even in trials, you will see God's love, and it will give you the power to withstand anything that comes your way.

I will be straightforward with you. There is a tribulation, a day of trial for everyone, including you. The Bible talks about the time of Jacob's trouble in Jeremiah 30:7, which says, *"Alas, for that day is great, so that none is like it: It is even the time of Jacob's trouble, but he shall be saved out of it."*

When that day comes, will you still be standing?

The answer to that question is dependent on your intake of God's Word, and meditation is the path that can get you there.

• CHAPTER 12 •

Stand Firm

It is essential to saturate your minds and thoughts with holy things. Feeding your spirit with the words of God will not only build your faith, but it will also make you contented.

Take a moment and imagine that you have everything in this world—billions of dollars in your account, airplanes, big businesses, fame, and popularity, but you don't have Jesus. Then, my friend, you don't have anything. On the other hand, if you don't have the billions, private jets, and businesses, but you have Jesus—rejoice and shout Hallelujah because you have everything!

Do you remember the story of Lazarus and the rich man?

Luke 16 talks about Lazarus, a poor man who lay outside the gate of a rich man's home. Lazarus was so destitute he hoped "to eat what fell from the rich man's table," but the rich man was very unsympathetic to Lazarus, offering him no help or compassion. When they both died, Lazarus was welcomed into the Bosom of Abraham, while the rich man was condemned to hell.

Before proceeding, it's important to point out that Lazarus didn't make it to Abraham's bosom because he was poor — he made it because he was righteous. On the flip side, the rich man did not go to hell because he was rich — he was condemned to hell because he didn't know God.

In the end, the table was flipped, and the rich man couldn't even get a drop of water to cool his tongue from the tormenting flames, while the impoverished one had everything he wanted.

The story of Lazarus and the rich man shows us how short life on earth is. Our earthly life is so short, like a dot in eternity. However, what we do in this short time will determine the life we live eternally.

If you look around, you will see people planning everything, trying so hard to grab up everything they can in this earth. They do this because they lack wisdom. The Bible says in Psalm 74:20, *"The dark places of the earth are full of the habitations of cruelty.* Just turn on the television or walk down the street, and you will see many resorting to wickedness to have a better life here on Earth – but God is calling you to think differently.

He's calling you to change your mindset and to pay more attention to the Word. He said, *"My son, attend to my words; incline thine ear unto my sayings. Let them not depart from thine eyes; keep them in the midst of thine heart. For they are life unto those that find them, and health to all their flesh."* Proverbs 4:20–22

God is telling us to keep His words in our hearts and meditate on them so we can survive in these times.

It doesn't matter what you are going through. Hold onto the Word.

Hold on, and don't give up.

In moments like these, I always think about Shadrach, Meshach, and Abednego. In the face of death, their response to the king was, *"O Nebuchadnezzar, we are not careful to answer thee in this matter. If it be so, our God whom we serve is able to deliver us from the burning fiery furnace, and he will deliver us out of thine hand, O king. But if not, be it known unto thee, O king, that we will not serve thy gods, nor worship the golden image which thou hast set up"* Daniel 3:16–18.

Shadrach, Meshach, and Abednego made up their minds that they were not bowing down even if it cost them their lives. They knew that if God didn't save them, they would have gone to heaven, and that should also be your mentality.

Yes. God can bring you out of your predicament. He's able to save and deliver you, but if He doesn't, DO NOT go against the Word of God.

Remember, only those that hold on to God's Word and stand in God's Word will make it in these last days.

Jesus said, "*Lord said, Simon, Simon, behold, Satan hath desired to have you, that he may sift you as wheat: But I have prayed for thee, that thy faith fail not: and when thou art converted, strengthen thy brethren.*" Luke 22:31–32

Today, I pray that your faith will not fail but that you find the strength to withstand every persecution or tribulations that may come your way.

I pray that your faith will not waver and that the Word of God will gain grounds in your heart, so even in the trials of life, you stand firm and hold on to God's Word against all the odds.

I pray that when all the dust has settled, you will remain standing in the name of Jesus.

Hallelujah!

ABOUT THE AUTHOR

Isaac Samuel II is the senior pastor of Check It Church International, a ministry committed to providing Christians with sound Bible teaching through weekly sermons, e-services, live events, and resource materials and books. Pastor Isaac is also the CEO of Check It Clothing, an anointed Christian apparel line.

www.ingramcontent.com/pod-product-compliance
Lightning Source LLC
Chambersburg PA
CBHW071036080526
4458 7CB00015B/2639